Praise for *Today You Will*

"Despite devastation and despair, we have a choice this day to live *better* rather than *bitter*. Ian's life is a profoundly inspiring reminder that when we chose better, we find hope! If faith is the hallmark of our Christian heritage, evidence of that inheritance is an indomitable spirit to persevere. Ian's life offers us a legacy of hope because he chose to live better!"

Rick Rigsby, PhD
President, Rick Rigsby Communications
Motivational Speaker, Minister & Best-Selling Author
Lessons From a Third Grade Dropout

"I often say that 'to whom much is given, much is expected.' This book is a powerful reminder that one of the greatest gifts we receive is the day right in front of us. *Today You Will* challenges us to stop delaying what matters most and to recognize the responsibility—and opportunity—we carry each day we are blessed with another breath. Brian's message is thoughtful, honest, and profoundly inspiring. He invites us to use what we've been given to not only live with purpose, but to make a difference—starting today."

David G. Voss, Jr.
Executive Chairman, Miron Construction Co., Inc.

"Today You Will is a powerful reminder of how precious life is and how intentional living begins with presence. Through the stories of Ezra and Ian, Brian Rasmussen shows that truth is revealed when we honor today, engage in continual self-work, and live faithfully with the people and purposes entrusted to us."

Barb LaMue
Former President & CEO, New North, Inc.

"Today You Will blends a compelling story with a practical framework you can act on now. The five principles move you from 'someday' to 'today' — where every real outcome is created."

Scott Bushkie
Managing Partner & Founder, Cornerstone Business Services
Author, *Finish Strong: Sell Your Business On Your Terms*

"A page-turning retelling of a pivotal spiritual conversation. A compelling invitation to leverage this present moment. A heart-felt tribute to a son who died so young. *Today You Will* is all of this and so much more. Few authors weave together poetry, clarity, and humility like Brian does in this book as he urges all of us to honor each and every day that God has given to us."

Mike Novotny
Lead Speaker, Time of Grace
Author, *Taboo: Topics Christians Should Be Talking About But Don't*

"Brian embraces the truth that we are not defined by what broke us, but by the courage that rises from our scars and turns every regret into the first line of redemption."

Josh Dunn
President & Founder, Premier Media

"As individuals, we all long for understanding and fulfillment, yet often feel overwhelmed by where to begin. In *Today You Will*, Brian Rasmussen offers a clear and practical roadmap for living and leading a more purposeful life — one that begins with being present today. This book reminds us that real change isn't about dramatic leaps, but about embracing where we are and taking steady steps forward, trusting each day as a sacred opportunity for growth, grace, and redemption."

Bret Salscheider
President & CEO, YMCA of the Fox Cities

Today You Will

*A Story of Redemption, Courage,
and 5 Principles to a Better You*

Brian Rasmussen

Today Leadership Press

Appleton, Wisconsin (USA)

Today You Will

A Story of Redemption, Courage,
and 5 Principles to a Better You

ISBN: 979-8-9944978-0-7

Published by:
Today Leadership Press
Appleton, Wisconsin (USA)

Dedication

This book is dedicated to my son, Ian —
a wise son whose courage, faith, and grace continue
to shape our lives and bear fruit in others.

To my wife, Jill, and our children,
Hilary, Hannah, and Noah —
your love and dedication were the strength that carried us,
even when the way forward was unclear.

And to all who walked with us — through presence, prayer,
care, and compassion — this story bears witness to what
love makes possible.

Foreword

Brian Rasmussen nails it.

This is a must-read. A life changer — or maybe I should say, a life *enricher*. It's encouraging, it's engaging, and it will move you forward toward the person you want to be... and hope to be.

Can I use the name of the book in a sentence? **"Today I will... start reading** *Today You Will*.**"**

I promise you won't regret it. And because of it, you may find yourself carrying fewer regrets in life.

Don't wait. The stories will draw you in and show you what truly matters. They don't just inspire — they give you tools. Tools to move toward what you want out of life. Don't put off until tomorrow what matters today.

I've been known for saying, *"Live life to the fullest."* If that's your desire — through the good times *and* the hard times — then this book is for you.

Today You Will is fantastically written. It's personal. It's practical. It's grounded in great principles, and it's an enjoyable, meaningful read. It takes you into the past — even into biblical times — helps you be present today, and gives you hope for the future.

Well done, Brian. Well done.

Bob Lenz
Founder & President, Lifest

Contents

Introduction

Before You Begin

Most of us do not intend to drift.
We intend to grow.
We intend to improve.
We intend to change the things we know are
not working.

And yet, somehow, intention alone rarely carries us
where we hoped to go.

Life becomes busy.
Responsibilities multiply.
Disappointments leave marks.
Time moves faster than we expect.

And gradually — almost quietly — we learn how to live without pursuing what we once desired.

This book is not written for people who lack desire. It is written for people who feel it — and have delayed responding to it.

If you are holding this book, chances are there is time to consider what's ahead.

What you have wanted.

What you feel is unfinished.
Unresolved.

Not broken beyond repair —
just not where you hoped it would be by now.

You may not be able to name it precisely.
But you feel it.

A conversation you've avoided.
A habit you've learned to tolerate.
A calling you once felt clearly — and now you keep it at arm's length.
A version of yourself you believed you would become … eventually.

This book does not ask you to change everything.
It does not demand dramatic promises.
It does not shame delay.

Instead, it asks something gentler — and far
more honest:

What will you do with the day you have been given
today?

The pages ahead begin with a story — not advice.
A story about a man who waited too long.
A man who made choices that narrowed his future.
A man who believed change had passed him by.

His name is Ezra.

You will meet him not at the beginning of his life, but
near the end —
at a moment when time feels painfully limited and
clarity arrives too late.

Or so it seems.

Ezra's story is not meant to frighten you.
It is meant to help you pause.
To reflect.
To recognize yourself without condemnation.

Today You Will

Because whether our circumstances are dramatic or
ordinary, most change is delayed for the same reason:

We believe we still have time.

Time to prepare.
Time to feel ready.
But life does not always wait for our timing to be right.
It waits for our honesty.

And sometimes, the most important work begins not
when we feel prepared —
but when we finally stop postponing what we already
know matters.

You do not need to read this book quickly.
You do not need to agree with everything
you encounter.
You do not need to make promises as you begin.

All that is asked of you is to be present.

To read slowly.
To notice what resonates.
To pay attention to the places where something stirs
within you —
when you quietly say, *This is for me.*

Because those moments — the subtle ones — are often invitations.

The story you are about to read leads into principles, not prescriptions.
Into reflection, not formulas.
Into movement that happens one choice at a time.

And these principles are not meant to be mastered once and left behind.
They are meant to accompany you.

You may find yourself coming back to a single chapter.
To a single idea.
To a single pledge —
allowing its words to steady you again.

This book is meant to be a companion, not a checklist.

It ends not with a command, but with a reminder:

That today is not insignificant.
That today is not wasted.
That today still holds possibility.

You do not have to know every detail for the journey that lies ahead.
You only need to be willing to honor the day you have already been given.

Ezra's story begins now.

Before it does, take a moment.
Breathe.
Notice where you are.

This book is not focused on changing your life all at
once.
It is asking you to consider what might happen
if you stopped waiting
and allowed *today* to matter.

Ezra's Story

Chapter 1

The Cell and the Light

A pale light trembled upon the wall.

It came not from the sun itself but from some distant opening above the wall, a narrow slit through which morning fought its way into the cold cell.

The light crept across the rough floor like a living thing, touching chains, a drinking bowl, and the torn edge of the prisoner's sleeve.

Then it reached Ezra's face.

He did not move at first.

Sleep had not truly claimed him during the night — only a kind of waiting, an uneasy drift between memory and dread. He opened his eyes to the same shadows he had closed them to and wondered, Is this the day?

Somewhere beyond the walls, water dripped steadily, like an anxious heartbeat in the silence. From the corridor came the low scrape of a guard's footsteps, then quiet again. Ezra listened to it all, afraid even of the sound of his own breath.

Across from him, Malek lay curled against the far wall, his back to the light. Ezra could tell by the rhythm of the man's breathing that he still slept. The chains between them rattled softly whenever Malek shifted. Ezra stared at the iron links that joined them and thought how strange it was — to be bound in this way to the very man who had led him here.

He turned his face to the wall and closed his eyes, but the images would not rest: the dark alley, sudden lights, shouting, the impact that drove him to the ground. The trial. The sentence. The laughter.

A tremor passed through him.

He pressed his palms to his face and whispered, "God… if you still hear me…"

But no words followed. What could he ask for? A miracle? A delay? Forgiveness?

Forgiveness was for the righteous, not for someone like him.

The light on the floor grew stronger. Ezra watched it climb the wall, saw the color of day seep into the cell. Morning was coming — and with it, whatever awaited him today. He had seen the preparations the day before: the gathering of guards, the talk of a "special" execution and the statement that certain prisoners would pay for their debts come sunrise. But none of the prisoners were told who would be taken or when. That ignorance was its own kind of torture.

He rubbed his wrists where the iron had worn the skin raw and thought of the sun beyond the walls — of people waking in the upper streets, washing their hands, calling to one another. Somewhere above, he could hear the muffled sounds of the city — merchants raising their shutters, women grinding grain, the faint cry of a rooster.

Today You Will

The world still goes on, he thought bitterly. Even when a man's world ends.

He drew his knees to his chest and tried to remember another morning — one from long ago, when the air smelled of bread instead of iron.

Chapter 2

The Days of Youth

He was twelve again, running through the narrow alleys of his village near Jericho, his feet dusty, his heart alive. His mother's voice echoed behind him, calling him back for morning prayers. He had been late again, distracted by the stonecutter's shop and the sound of hammer on chisel.

The craftsman had smiled at the boy's curiosity and said, "You have hands made for shaping, not stealing."

He remembered laughing then, promising that one day he would build something that lasted.

Today You Will

But that was before he met Malek.

Malek had come into his life like a storm. He was older by a few years, sharper in tongue and quicker in confidence. Ezra had admired him instantly — his way of speaking, his boldness, the way others seemed to listen when he entered a room.

Malek taught him small things at first: how to talk a merchant down, how to slip a coin unnoticed from a crowded table, how to laugh when caught so that people thought it was all a jest. Ezra had hesitated the first time, but Malek's laughter was infectious, his charm irresistible.

"Why should the rich have everything?" Malek would say. "We only take what they will not miss."

And Ezra, foolish in youth, had believed him.

One night, under the stars, they spoke of dreams. Ezra had confessed he wanted to see Jerusalem — the great city of their fathers — and stand in the temple courts. Malek had smiled in that secret way of his.

"Then come with me," he said. "There's more to see there than priests and prayers."

***

The memory shifted like smoke — years passing in the span of a breath. The markets of Jerusalem. The taverns. The deals made in shadows. Ezra's skill had grown, but his peace had not. With each theft came a smaller portion of laughter, and a heavier burden on his conscience.

He had thought of leaving Malek more than once, but there was always another promise, another plan, another chance to "make it big." And beneath it all, the strange loyalty of shared sins — two men too deep in their own lies to walk apart.

Then came the night that ended it all: the failed robbery, the soldiers' torches, the running through alleys slick with rain. Malek had fallen, and Ezra had turned back to help him — only to be seized by the guards as Malek fled.

But Malek had been caught too, later that same night. And when the soldiers demanded names, Malek had spoken Ezra's first.

Chapter 3

The Longest Morning

Ezra was stirred from the memory by a bitter laugh.

"Ezra? You prayin'?" Malek muttered.
"Keeps me awake."

Ezra said nothing.

Malek stretched, the chains clinking softly. "Old friend, you worry too much. Maybe it isn't us today."

Ezra met his gaze. "And if it is?"

Malek shrugged. "Then we'll face it like men. It's only pain. And it ends soon enough."

He turned away again, yawning, as though the matter were settled. Ezra watched him in disbelief — at the calmness, the arrogance that had once drawn him in and now repulsed him.

He sank to the floor, his back to the wall.

Even now, chained to the same wall, Malek appeared to slip back into sleep, as though guilt were a burden only the weak carried.

How can he take this so lightly?

Ezra envied him — and hated himself for envying him.

***

Time passed. The cell grew warmer. The light on the wall shifted from gold to white. From somewhere above came a sudden sound — trumpets, faint but clear. Then shouts. Ezra looked up, straining to hear. The voices were too distant to make out the words, but the tone was unmistakable: excitement, urgency.

"Another festival crowd," Malek murmured. "They celebrate while we rot."

Ezra thought of the stories told by his mother describing the pilgrims arriving from every corner of Judea, bringing their lambs for sacrifice, singing the old songs of deliverance. Passover, he realized. The day of remembering how God had set their fathers free.

The irony struck him hard.

Freedom. While I wait to die.

He closed his eyes and whispered, "Mother, I hope you don't see me now."

Her face rose before him, clear as the day she had spoken words of belief in him.

Chapter 4

The Making of a Thief

The memory came to him not as a single picture, but as a weight.

It pressed upon his chest the way guilt presses on a man who's learned to live without calling it by its name.

Ezra saw himself, younger — yet already tired.

He was standing outside his mother's doorway, listening to her hum a psalm while she mended an old cloak by candlelight. She had always been the one who believed he could be better. "You have your father's eyes," she used to say, "and if you ever learn to see with your heart, those eyes will lead you well."

But Ezra had not come to listen that night. He had come to avoid her eyes.

He slipped past her quickly and carefully exited through the narrow doorway, his purse heavy with coins that were not his.

Inside a nearby tavern, Malek waited — seated in the shadowed corner of the room, laughing as he counted their latest take.

"See, brother?" Malek grinned. "They won't miss it. The wealthy never do."

Ezra didn't laugh. Not at first. He stared at the coins as though they might accuse him.

But Malek's voice was a soothing poison.

"You worry too much. You think they ever worried about us when we were hungry? Look around — this is how the world works. The strong take, the weak get taken."

Ezra tried to answer, but his throat closed. He wanted to say that his mother prayed differently.

Instead, he swallowed hard and said, "Maybe you're right."

And with those words, something inside him shifted.

***

The days that followed blurred together — a slow slide from unease into numbness.

The thefts grew bolder. The justifications came quicker.

Each new wrong required a smaller lie to cover the last. He began to avoid his brother Eli, who had once been his closest friend.

Eli tried to talk sense into him one evening. "Ezra, this isn't who you are. You don't have to keep doing this."

Ezra had wanted, so desperately, to confess right there — to say, I don't know how to stop.

But pride rose like a shield.

"What do you know of it?" he snapped. "You live by rules written for other men — men who never had to fight for bread."

Eli looked at him a long moment and said quietly, "No, brother. I live by rules that keep me from becoming the kind of man who forgets who he is."

That sentence haunted Ezra for years.

But back then, he had only scoffed, pretending it didn't matter.

He turned away and found comfort in the only voice that didn't make him feel small — Malek's.

Malek became the echo Ezra chose to believe.

Whenever his conscience stirred, Malek drowned it out. Ezra started to measure worth by cunning.

He stole not only from strangers but from those who trusted him — a merchant who had given him work, a neighbor who had shared his bread.

And when his mother's eyes, soft and sorrowful, asked if he was all right, he lied to her too.

Each lie built another wall.

Each excuse laid another stone in the prison of his own making.

Until one day, Ezra could no longer feel the shame.

He felt only the dull safety of not caring.

Chapter 5

The Footsteps

The sound of boots broke the silence. Heavy, deliberate. The corridor filled with echoes. Malek sat up. Ezra felt his stomach turn cold.

The key scraped in the lock. The door creaked open. A guard entered — the tall one with the scar across his cheek.

"Up," he barked at Malek. "You're coming with us."

Malek smirked. "Both of us?"

The guard's eyes were flat. "Both."

Chains rattled. Hands grasped. Ezra stumbled as they pulled him to his feet. The sunlight in the corridor blinded him after the long darkness.

They were led through a passage that climbed toward daylight, the air growing fresher, the sounds of the city swelling. Ezra blinked as they emerged into the courtyard. The scent of dust and olive wood filled his lungs.

Soldiers were assembling there — several of them, armed and ready. And beyond the gate, a crowd waited. The murmuring of hundreds of voices, the restless movement of people shifting for a better view.

Ezra's breath caught.

So it is today.

Beside him, Malek gave a low whistle. "Quite an audience," he said.

Ezra said nothing. His gaze had fixed upon something else — a third man standing nearby, flanked by guards. His face was bruised, his robe torn, a crown of thorns pressed cruelly upon his head. Yet there was something in the man's bearing — a strange calm, a quiet dignity that made the noise of the crowd seem distant and unreal.

The man turned slightly, and for a moment their eyes met.

Ezra felt as though the world itself had gone still.

There was no accusation in those eyes, no hatred, not even pity — only a depth that seemed to see through him, past the chains, past the guilt, to something he had forgotten existed.

And in that single moment, without knowing why, Ezra felt both fear and hope rise within him together — twin flames in the darkness of his soul.

***

The guards shouted. The beams were lifted.

The procession began.

And as they led him through the gates into the blinding

morning, Ezra whispered the same words that had haunted his dreams through the long night:

"How did I come to this?"

Chapter 6

The Road

The air outside struck Ezra like a wave.

It was warm already, and heavy with the mingled smells of dust, sweat, and smoke from the city's morning fires. After the dim chill of the cell, the light felt almost violent. He blinked hard, struggling to adjust as the guards pushed them forward into the street.

The noise was staggering.

Vendors shouted. Children darted through the crowd. The murmur of hundreds of voices rolled like surf against the narrow walls of the lane.

But beneath the ordinary sounds of the city pulsed something different today—an undercurrent of excitement, almost celebration. People pressed in from both sides as the soldiers marched the three prisoners forward.

Ezra could feel their eyes on him—some curious, some disgusted, others strangely eager, as though they'd been waiting for this spectacle all morning.

He wanted to shout that they were wrong about him, that he was not what they thought. But what would it change? The rope around his chest, the beam across his shoulders, the weight of his own guilt—those were the truest things he carried.

Malek walked just ahead of him, laughing low under his breath. "Look at them," he said. "They act like they've never seen a condemned man before."

Ezra didn't answer. His gaze had turned toward the third prisoner.

The man walked between them, silent. His body swayed under the burden of the rough-hewn beam the soldiers had placed across his back, yet his steps were steady.

The blood from the thorns on his forehead had dried into dark streaks along his cheeks, and the sunlight caught in them like iron. His robe was little more than a torn strip of linen, clinging to skin marked by lashes.

And yet — there was no anger in him.

No pleading, no defiance. Only a strange composure, as though the suffering itself had become a path he had already chosen.

Ezra could not stop watching him. Every now and then the man would stumble, and the soldiers would shout, striking him with their rods. Each time, he would fall to his knees, catch his breath, and rise again without a word.

At one such fall, Ezra heard himself whisper, "Let him rest."

A guard swung his staff toward him. "You'll speak when spoken to, thief."

The wood caught Ezra in the ribs, and he staggered, gasping. Malek laughed again.

"Careful, Ezra," he said. "You'll draw their kindness away from me."

But the man in the middle turned at the sound of the blow. Their eyes met once more. For an instant, Ezra felt that same disarming calm as in the courtyard—an understanding deeper than pity. The man said nothing, yet something in that gaze felt like forgiveness itself.

Ezra dropped his eyes and walked on, ashamed without knowing why.

Chapter 7

The Street of Olive Sellers

The procession wound through the narrow streets, climbing gradually toward the western gate. At each corner, more people joined the stream. Some jeered. Some spat. Others whispered to one another in tones too low for Ezra to hear.

A group of women stood near a doorway, their faces veiled. One of them reached out as the silent man passed. Her hand brushed his arm, trembling. Ezra saw her lips move, but her words were swallowed by the noise. The man looked at her and nodded once—slowly, almost tenderly—and she wept aloud.

Ezra could not understand it.

Why should a stranger's sorrow pierce him more deeply than the rod? Why did the world seem to tilt around this man, as though every sound and shadow bent toward him?

He tried to shake the feeling. He was a fool to think of anything but survival. And yet, in the chaos of the crowd, he found himself studying the man's back, the rhythmic rise and fall of his shoulders beneath the beam.

There was something familiar there, though he could not place it—something that stirred the memory of prayers he had long forgotten.

Chapter 8

The Turning

As they neared the gate, the streets widened, and the city's hum gave way to open air. The wind carried the smell of dry grass and distant stone. Ahead lay a hill, barren and sharp against the pale sky.

Ezra felt his knees weaken. He knew now where they were being taken.

He had seen that place once before, from afar — the place of public execution outside the city walls. The place the soldiers called the Skull.

His stomach turned.

He glanced at Malek, whose grin had finally faded.

"This is it," Malek muttered. "So much for your prayers."

Ezra said nothing. His mouth had gone dry. The heat pressed down like a weight.

The guards shouted again, ordering them to quicken their pace. Ezra stumbled forward, the wood digging into his shoulders. His breath came in ragged bursts. All around him the crowd surged, their voices rising — mockery, laughter, curses.

Somewhere in the din he heard a single cry, clear and pleading:

"Let him go! He has done nothing wrong!"

Ezra turned his head toward the voice, but the soldiers pushed him onward.

The man in the middle fell again. This time he did not rise immediately. The beam slipped from his back and struck the stones with a hollow sound.

The soldiers cursed and struck him, but he did not move. Ezra watched, horror growing in his chest. Blood streamed down the man's side. His hands trembled weakly against the ground.

A stranger stepped out from the crowd — broad-shouldered, dark-skinned, a foreigner by his dress. The soldiers seized him, forcing him to lift the fallen beam. The man obeyed, bewildered but silent. He bore the weight and followed beside the prisoner, carrying what the other could no longer carry.

Ezra's throat tightened.

Who is he? he wondered. What kind of man commands such mercy from strangers?

They resumed the climb.

Chapter 9

The Hill

The hill rose steep and gray, stripped of trees. The wind was stronger here, whipping the dust into small spirals. From its crest, the city spread out below them, glittering in the sun.

Ezra's legs trembled with exhaustion. Each step felt heavier than the last. When they reached the top, the guards shouted for them to halt.

And then Ezra saw the posts.

Three of them—rough beams already set in the ground, their shadows stretching long and thin across the earth.

At their bases lay the tools: hammers, nails, ropes.

A sound escaped him, half gasp, half moan. He had heard stories, but seeing it now turned his stomach to stone.

Beside him, Malek cursed under his breath.

"So this is how it ends."

Ezra looked again at the silent man. He stood between them still, head bowed, face streaked with blood and dust. Yet even now, there was no fear in him. Only weariness—and something else Ezra could not name.

The soldiers began their grim work. Ezra heard the clang of metal, the barked orders. Two guards approached him, seizing his arms. He fought instinctively, twisting, shouting, "Please—don't—"

But over his cries rose another voice—soft, low, like a breath carried on the wind.

"Father, forgive them... for they know not what they do."

Ezra froze.

The words hung in the air, too calm, too steady to belong in such a place.

He turned his head. The man was looking upward, his lips barely moving. His voice trembled not with fear but with compassion, as though he pitied the very ones who tortured him.

Ezra stared, breathless. Something broke inside him— some hard, cold place he had kept sealed for years.

Chapter 10

The Cross

The sky darkened slightly, as if a cloud had passed before the sun. Ezra felt his wrists bound, the rope burning his skin. The hammer's first blow sent fire through his arm, and he cried out.

When they lifted the beams, he heard the crowd again—their mocking laughter, their cruel jokes. Some hurled taunts.

"Save yourself, Chosen One."

But beneath it all, there was a sound like weeping. A woman's voice.

Ezra forced his eyes open and turned his head toward the man in the center.

The cross stood higher than the others, silhouetted against the white blaze of noon. The man hung there, his head bowed, his body trembling. A few women knelt at his feet, and among them a young man stood, his face streaked with tears.

Malek's voice broke through the din — muttering curses between gasps of pain.

"If you are so holy," he spat toward the center, "then save yourself — and us!"

He then encouraged Ezra to join his mockery.

Instinctively, Ezra was about to comply but the inner voice which he had suppressed so many times before when directed by Malek just spoke, "Enough, Malek... STOP!"

The words pierced the air like light through darkness.

Ezra felt them reverberate deep within him—past fear, past agony, past all the guilt that had weighed his soul for years.

Then Ezra's eyes met the eyes of the man on the center cross. There was no condemnation there, no triumph—only peace.

And in that peace, Ezra had hope.

This was no ordinary prisoner.

No thief. No rebel. No madman.

This was the One the prophets had spoken of.

The One his mother had prayed to.

Tears began to blur his vision. His breath came in shallow gasps.

He whispered, barely audible, "Remember me... when You come into Your kingdom."

For a moment, the world fell utterly silent.

Then the answer came — gentle, certain, eternal: "Truly, today you will be with me in paradise."

Ezra closed his eyes.

The pain did not vanish, but it no longer owned him. He felt the weight of the world lift, replaced by something vast and quiet.

The wind rose, cool against his face.

Somewhere far below, the city's noise faded into stillness.

And in that stillness, Ezra — once a thief, now forgiven — finally understood what it meant to live... even as he died.

~ The End ~

The Transition

Ezra's Story Into Your Story

You have just walked with Ezra through the final hours of his life, and I am honored you stayed with him until the end. His story lingers because — whether we admit it out loud or not — it is our story. I know this because it has been my story too. Every one of us carries places where we shine and places where we stumble. Being human means living somewhere between what we are and what we long to become.

We often find ourselves like Ezra — hesitating on the threshold of change. We ache for "more," yet we delay. We imagine a different life, but we do not step toward it. We doubt our ability. We justify our inaction. We hide instead of asking for help.

I know this pattern well. I lived it while writing this book. Ezra's story was placed on my heart years ago, and though the message felt urgent, I avoided it. I thought about it constantly, but I did not act. I kept believing "one day" would be the right time. And I postponed what mattered most… again and again.

Then life changed in a way I could never have predicted.

My son, Ian, was diagnosed with stage-four renal medullary carcinoma — an aggressive cancer primarily found in young people with the sickle-cell trait. It is rare, brutal, and notoriously resistant to treatment. When we asked the doctor what we should expect, he told us that most who face this diagnosis do not survive. His words proved devastatingly true. Ian's battle ended in six months.

That chapter of this book — his chapter — will come at the end. It is where I will honor him and share the lessons he taught us, including one that now sits at the very center of this book:

The importance of today.

After hearing his diagnosis, Ian chose to live with a fierce simplicity. *One day at a time.* He understood, in a way many of us never do, that today is the only day anyone truly receives. Today is the gift. Today is the chance. Today is the moment with weight.

And so I urge you — gently but earnestly — to consider the preciousness of the day you have been given right now. Not tomorrow's hypothetical hours. Not the fantasy of a "better season." Today.

See yourself in Ezra's hesitation. See yourself in the places you've put off improvement. See yourself in the longing that will not quiet. And then listen closely to the same words Jesus spoke to Ezra:

"Today you will."

Not later.
Not eventually.
Not when it is convenient or comfortable.

Today.

To help you live into that promise, the next five chapters introduce the framework that will guide you toward your preferred future. In the story, Ezra had only one "today" left. You and I — at least for now — are still being given more.

These five principles are designed to help you honor each day with intention, humility, and courage.

They follow the letters of the word **TODAY**:

T — Tell Yourself What You Want
O — Own the Outcomes
D — Design a Life Plan
A — Acknowledge the Gaps
Y — You Are the Investment

These principles are not meant to be mastered once and left behind.

They are meant to accompany you — because every *today* brings different questions, different challenges, and different opportunities for growth.

Let's walk into these principles together — and make the most of the day you have right now.

Today you will.

Principle #1

Tell Yourself What You Want

Desire is the Spark That Begins Every Journey of Change

There comes a moment in every life when the heart whispers what the mouth has forgotten to say—a moment when life shifts from drifting to direction. It is the moment when your soul, worn from silence, finally admits: **I want more than this.**

Ezra felt this long before he met Jesus. Even after years of quieting his inner voice, the longing for a different life never fully died. **Desire rarely does.** When a heart becomes honest enough, desire rises again and finds its voice.

You may feel as though you have muted that whisper. Life fills our days with responsibilities, distractions, obligations, and the noise of others' expectations. Somewhere along the way, the voice that once said, *"What if...?"* begins to say, *"Why bother?"*

But the truth is still there, waiting.

It waits beneath the surface like a buried ember — small, but alive.

If you allow yourself even a moment of stillness, you will hear it again.

**Recognizing what you want is not arrogance.
It is honesty.**

And honesty is where every new story begins.

Being honest with yourself — humble enough to name the truth — is the first step in freeing yourself from whatever has held you back. Before you can change, you must dare to desire the life you were created for. Before you can travel the road toward it, you must tell yourself what you want.

The Heart of the Principle

Telling yourself what you want is not about crafting slogans or shouting declarations into the air. It is allowing the message deep within you to be expressed. It is speaking the desire that was placed in your heart long before fear taught you to silence it.

Desire reveals direction.
Desire creates movement.

When you dare to say what you desire — even privately — something shifts:

Your heart begins to rise.
Your mind starts searching for ways to honor that longing.
Your spirit — perhaps weary from years of waiting — begins to wake up.

Most people do not fail to change because they lack talent or worth. They fail because they never permit themselves to confess what they truly want.

But the truth remains:

You cannot reach the future you desire if you never name it.

When you tell yourself what you want, it becomes your compass — orienting you toward the person you were created to be. Naming your desire does not guarantee immediate attainment, but it creates the alignment that draws you out of hiding and sets your face toward the horizon again.

———————

The Inner Battle

There is always a tug-of-war between longing and fear. Always.

That is why this principle may appear simple, yet proves so difficult. Not because you do not know what you want, but because you are afraid to admit it.

Ezra spent years suppressing what he knew in his heart was true. Perhaps you have done something similar. Maybe you have known disappointment. Maybe someone belittled your hopes. Maybe past failures have conditioned you to expect less. Maybe fear has convinced you that wanting "more" is dangerous.

You may find yourself wondering:
- What if I'm wrong?
- What if I try and fail again?
- What if wanting exposes my vulnerability?
- What if people don't understand?
- What if it's too late?

These questions are normal. They visit everyone who has ever dared to change.

But desire is not the enemy. It is the invitation.

If you think back on the most important moments of your life, they all began with courage wrapped in uncertainty. You didn't take the next step because you knew everything.

You took it because you were finally honest about what you wanted.

Naming what you want brings your hope out of the shadows and into the light. It takes the longing that has lived behind your ribs and allows it to breathe again.

The Role of Others

**Even the strongest hearts need companions —
wise voices, trusted eyes, steady hands.**

Your desired future is too important to walk toward alone.

Not because you are incapable, but because desire, once spoken, must be guarded... protected... encouraged.

Ezra was shaped for years by Malek, a voice that distorted his desires rather than clarifying them. You and I must choose differently.

Speaking your desire is essential for forming a clear vision of the future. But at some point, you will need someone you trust — someone capable of listening past your fears and hearing the deeper truth in your voice.

A trusted advisor is not meant to define your desire for you. **But they *can* help uncover truth with you.**

They can help you recognize what resonates with your spirit and what does not. They can help sift through noise and steady your focus. They can help protect the fragile beginnings of hope when old doubts try to pull you back.

You do not need to announce your longing to the whole world. But you should not hide it from those who are meant to help you rise.

Naming Desire is the Beginning of Transformation

Something powerful happens when you finally tell yourself what you want:

Shame loosens its grip.
Fear loses authority.
Hope begins to breathe.
The future starts to feel possible again.

You stop living only by memory
and start living by intention.

This is the beginning of your turning point—your shift from "someday" into "today."

When you tell yourself what you want, your words
begin shaping your future the way a seed shapes
a harvest.

Heaven listens when you speak the truth.
Your heart listens, too.

Naming your desire is honesty.
Naming it is the first act of faith.
And it is the first step toward the future God is inviting
you into.

———————

TODAY YOU WILL PLEDGE

Principle #1: Tell Yourself What You Want

(Hear this as truth spoken over your life today.)

Today is the day you reclaim your voice —

the day you step away from the shadows of "someday"

and stand in the light of "today."

The day you speak honestly about the future
you desire —

not with arrogance, but with courage.

You are allowed to desire a life aligned with the purpose
placed within you.

Your longing is not foolish — it is the echo of who you
were made to become.

The One who formed you has shaped your future with
intention

and has planted good desires that long to rise.

You are free to name the hope that lives beneath your
fear.

You are free to speak aloud the future you have carried
in silence.

You are free to pursue the vision calling you forward.

Today You Will

Embrace the desire that draws you toward the light,

and protect it with the help of those who believe in your becoming.

Trust that the God who began this work in you

will guide your steps as you rise.

Take the first step forward.

Tell yourself what you want.

Today you will.

Principle #2

Own the Outcomes

Ownership Begins By Taking Responsibility

There comes a moment in every story — Ezra's, mine, yours — when we can no longer let yesterday steer tomorrow. A moment when we stop blaming the wind, the season, or the circumstances and finally admit: *my hands have been on the wheel.*

Owning the outcomes of your life is not about fault or shame.

It is about dignity—about standing in the light of truth and realizing that your preferred future becomes possible only when you choose responsibility for the steps that lead toward it.

Few realizations are more freeing than this:

Your life moves in the direction of your ownership.

To own the outcomes is to gently pull your life away from chance, excuse, and drift, and place it deliberately back into your care.

The Reality of Cause and Effect

Every life, whether we notice it or not, operates within a pattern of cause and effect.

Ezra didn't see this in his early years.

He believed his compromises harmed only himself.

He thought following Malek into darkness would cost no one but him.

But life has never worked that way.
We influence more than we imagine —
in both directions: toward harm or toward good.

Owning the outcomes is acknowledging:

My life is moving in the direction of my decisions.

If you want your tomorrow to look different, you must take ownership of the outcomes your life is producing today.

The Ripple Effect of Your Life

Every decision you make sends a ripple
outward — gentle or strong, visible or unseen.

When you begin taking ownership of your choices, something remarkable happens:

You begin to notice how deeply your growth impacts others.

We often think about "outcomes" as something
personal: *my* joy, *my* peace, *my* future.

But outcomes rarely stay contained within one life.

Your courage steadies others.
Your healing encourages others.
Your clarity becomes someone else's relief.
Your transformation becomes someone else's invitation.

This principle is not meant to burden you.

It is meant to remind you of what is possible.

When you move toward your preferred future,
you do not travel alone.

Those who love you benefit from your progress.

Those who depend on you feel your strength.

Those who watch you may finally believe change
is possible for them as well.

The change you pursue is not only for you.

It is a blessing waiting to extend outward.

Why You Should Not Walk This Path Alone

Owning your outcomes does not mean trying to anticipate everything by yourself.

Change withers in secrecy, and courage can fade when left unguarded.

Trusted advisors—people you choose for their clarity, steadiness, and integrity—help you see what you may overlook. They remind you of who you are becoming. They help you notice outcomes that are emerging, both the hopeful ones *and* the ones that need attention.

They can shield you when needed.

They can help you see that not all outcomes can be easily predicted. Sometimes those closest to you may feel unsure when they witness your growth—not out of opposition, but simply because change is unfamiliar. Trusted supporters can help you navigate these dynamics with grace so your progress isn't slowed by misunderstanding or discouragement.

Ownership is your responsibility —
but it flourishes best in the company of wise voices.

———————————

Hope Appears When You Accept
Your Role in the Story

There is a unique strength that rises when you accept ownership of your outcomes.

You stop waiting for someone else to change your life.

You stop rehearsing the past as a reason to fear
the future.

You stop surrendering possibility to circumstance.

Ownership becomes motivation.

It becomes clarity.

It becomes the quiet power to choose differently today.

You begin shaping a tomorrow that brings better results
for you and others.

You move toward the mission woven into you long before you recognized it.

You bless others through the renewal happening within you.

Owning the outcomes will not place a pause in your story,

it places the purpose in your story.

———————————

TODAY YOU WILL PLEDGE

Principle #2: Own the Outcomes

(Receive this truth as a quiet declaration over your life today.)

Your choices matter, and they hold the power to shape a better future for you and for those connected to your life.

Your future is not predetermined,

and your past is not your prison.

Today You Will

You are capable of change, and your decisions can bring blessing to those you love.

The Author of your life places before you both courage and responsibility, inviting you to walk with intention and sow the seeds that lead to good.

You are called to steward today with honesty and strength.

Take responsibility for the direction of your steps.

You do not walk alone —

trusted voices will steady you,

and God's guidance will meet you as you move forward.

Trust that new fruit will grow from new choices.

Own the outcomes your life is creating for you...

and for those who walk with you.

Today you will.

Principle #3

Design a Life Plan

Direction Is Not Found — It Is Formed

After desire awakens and ownership settles in, the horizon looks different than it once did. What felt distant begins to draw nearer. What was fog, becomes shape. A quiet realization rises in the heart:

My future is too important to leave to chance.

Ezra never understood this early in his life. He drifted from day to day, letting others determine his direction. Without intention, he surrendered his path to the loudest influence—specifically Malek. And because he never shaped a direction of his own, he was swept into a life he never meant to live.

Many of us know this same pattern.

Not because we lack desire — but because we lack design.

We want change, but habit pulls us into the familiar. We imagine a better life, yet we return to routines that offer only more of the same. Hope flickers, but without structure, it cannot take root.

Designing a life plan is how your hope becomes a path.

It is the moment when vision takes form, when longing finds structure, when direction starts shaping "someday" into "today."

A plan does not restrict you.
A plan frees you to move with intention.

The Courage to Build
What You Once Thought Impossible

A life plan is not a rigid blueprint — it is a courageous choice to shape your days around what matters most. It is the quiet, steady act of saying:

"If this future is worth wanting, it is worth building."

Some resist planning because they fear disappointment.

Some avoid it because they fear responsibility.

Others simply feel overwhelmed by the thought of choosing a direction at all.

But the truth is tender and clear:

If you do not design your future intentionally, life will design it for you.

Obligations will fill your days. Demands will crowd out purpose. The urgent will overshadow the important. And yet, with even the simplest plan—a prayerful, thoughtful, intentional direction—everything begins to shift.

A wish hopes for a better tomorrow.

A plan begins shaping a better today.

Designing your future is an act of courage.

It is how impossible things begin to become possible.

Why Vision Must Be Shaped Into Structure

Vision alone is not enough.

Desire without structure is like a seed without soil — full of potential but unable to grow.

A life plan gives that potential a place to take root.

Designing a plan does not mean controlling every aspect of your future.

It means clarifying what you will pursue and what you will protect.

It means addressing what you will no longer allow and what you will avoid.

Your plan becomes the trellis your growth can cling to.

It anchors your days when distractions pull.

It helps you choose instead of merely react.

When you shape your life with intention, you begin to recognize patterns — what strengthens you, what drains you, what aligns with your calling, and what pulls you away from it.

Your future will be shaped by what you are willing to structure.

You Are Not Intended to Build Alone

Even the bravest hearts lose clarity in isolation.

Even the strongest minds need perspective.

Even the most determined souls can drift without wise support.

The myth of the self-made person is
simply that — a myth.

Every meaningful transformation is strengthened by the presence of others.

A trusted advisor, guide, or mentor brings three essential gifts:

1. Clarity When the Path Is Still Forming

There will be moments when the steps you are taking do not yet reveal the destination. You may wonder:

> *Is this really leading anywhere?*
> *Am I fooling myself?*
> *Should I turn back?*

A trusted guide—the kind who has walked a similar road—can reassure you:

"Stay the course. This path leads where you hope, even if you cannot see it yet."

Their experience provides confidence in the plan when your courage feels thin.

------

2. Insight Into Blind Spots and Pitfalls

Every person has blind spots — areas of life we cannot see clearly because habit or fear obscures them. A trusted advisor helps you recognize patterns that could derail your progress, helping you refine your plan before missteps become setbacks.

They help you discern which opportunities align with your direction and which temptations would pull you off course.

This is not control.

It is companionship, protection, and wisdom.

---

3. Balance That Prevents Success in One Area and Collapse in Another

It is possible to pursue one part of your life with great passion — career, dreams, personal growth — while neglecting another part that is equally essential.

Wise counsel helps you avoid the trap of succeeding publicly while failing privately.

They remind you that your marriage, your children, your health, your faith, and your purpose are all part of the same story.

A life plan is not about winning in one area, while losing in another.

It is about becoming whole in every area you value.

A Life Plan Creates the Momentum of Intention

Once you shape a life plan—once you dare to give structure to what matters—momentum begins to build. Not loudly at first, but quietly, steadily, faithfully.

You begin to walk differently.
You begin to see differently.
You begin to think differently.

Your choices become more deliberate. Your days become more meaningful. And your steps begin to match the life you are creating.

This is the quiet miracle of intention:

What you design with clarity, you begin to pursue with courage.

A plan is not a cage; it is a compass.
It does not demand perfection; it invites direction.

Your heart already knows where it wants to go. Your plan allows your feet to follow.

The future you desire takes shape when direction becomes intentional.

TODAY YOU WILL PLEDGE

Principle #3: Design a Life Plan

*(Hear this spoken over your life today
with clarity and compassion.)*

You were created with purpose, and your future deserves intention.

You are not meant to drift through your days.

You carry hope, and you are capable of clarity.

Lift your eyes to the horizon calling your name,
and dare to shape your life toward it.

Choose direction instead of reaction,
purpose instead of habit,
intention instead of drift.

Allow experienced guides to help you navigate the path ahead.

Welcome trusted voices who steady your steps and protect your growth.

Your future is too sacred to leave to chance.
Choose your direction with courage.
Shape your days with purpose.
Build a plan that honors who you are becoming.

Heaven delights in those who pursue what they were created to achieve.

Design a plan for the life you were intended to live.

Today you will.

Principle #4

Acknowledge the Gaps

Honesty Is the Doorway to Transformation

There comes a moment in every meaningful journey when the path ahead suddenly comes into focus — and with it, the honest distance between where you stand and where you hope to be.

That moment can feel both sobering and sacred.

Ezra experienced such a moment beside Jesus. For years he avoided the truth about who he had become. He numbed it. He ignored it. He defended it.

But in the presence of grace, he finally saw clearly. He recognized the gap between the man he was and the man he was created to be.

And instead of running from the truth, he turned toward it.

This is the heart of this principle.

Acknowledging the gaps is not about condemnation or despair.

It is about courageous clarity.

It is the moment you become honest with yourself— in a way that frees you to move forward.

The Gentle Strength of Truth

Many people fear examining the gaps in their life. They fear what they might find. They fear what it might require. They fear reopening old wounds, revisiting old regrets, or admitting where growth is still needed.

But here is a quiet, life-giving truth:

Acknowledgment is not punishment — it is permission.

Ezra did not experience redemption because he
perfected himself.

His situation changed because he finally acknowledged
the truth.

That same soil of honesty is where new life begins for
you, too.

A person who refuses to see their gaps remains trapped
by them.

But a person who bravely names their gaps can begin to
overcome them.

Acknowledging the gaps means noticing habits that
no longer serve you...
fears that limit you...
patterns that restrict you...
and the true obstacles that could keep you from
traveling from where you are to where you long to be.

Before you can bridge a gap, you must first be willing to see it.

———————————

From Where You Are to Where You're Going

When you tell yourself what you want, you name your desired future.

When you own the outcomes, you find the motivation to journey toward it.

Your life plan gives shape, direction, and intention to your steps.

And then comes this essential moment:

Acknowledging the gaps invites you to see the **honest distance** between point A and point B—between your current reality and your preferred future.

Some gaps are small, like a crack in the path.

You cross them with a few deliberate steps—adjusting a routine, setting a boundary, changing a daily choice.

Other gaps are wider.

They require more than intention.

They call for structure, commitment, and the willingness to build what does not yet exist.

Seeing these gaps clearly is not judgment.

It is simply an honest assessment of the road ahead.

When you acknowledge the gaps, you stop expecting instant arrival and start respecting the process.
You stop calling yourself a failure for not reaching your destination today and begin asking wiser questions about what must be built in order to move forward.

Some gaps exist because of past choices
or neglected seasons.

Others are not your fault at all — they are simply the natural distance between where you are and where **anyone** in your position would need to grow and develop.

Either way, the invitation is the same:

Do not deny the gap.

Name it — and begin to build the bridge that will carry you across.

Why You Cannot Walk This Road Alone

There is a reason athletes need coaches, entrepreneurs seek advisors, and apprentices walk with mentors:

You cannot see all of your own gaps.

Some are hidden by blind spots.
Some are softened by self-protection.
Some are tangled with old wounds.
Some feel so familiar that you barely recognize them as gaps at all.

We were never designed to walk the path
of transformation alone.

Trusted advisors can help you recognize which gaps require a simple step and which require a carefully built bridge. They help you discern where to invest your time, energy, and training so you are not overwhelmed by everything at once.

Their role is not to control your journey —
but to strengthen it.

They speak courage where fear once lived.

They remind you who you are when discouragement whispers.

They help you distinguish between conviction
and condemnation, between needed growth
and needless guilt.

Support does not weaken your journey.
Support strengthens your becoming.

Your gaps are easier to face when you are not facing them alone.

The Freedom Found in Seeing Clearly

Acknowledging your gaps is not an attack; it is
an awakening.

It is not a sign of failure; it is a sign of readiness.

You cannot change what you will not face.

But once you face it with humility and courage, change
becomes not only possible —
but likely.

There is relief in clarity.

There is strength in honesty.

There is peace in no longer pretending.

Once you acknowledge your gaps, the journey ahead
becomes clearer.

You are no longer traveling in the dark.

You are no longer fighting unseen obstacles.

You are no longer confusing reaction with reality.

You begin to live intentionally, not defensively.

You begin to choose growth, not stagnation.

You begin to welcome guidance, not retreat
into seclusion.

You begin to become the person you were capable
of becoming all along.

Ezra's story reminds us that even at the final edge of life,
clarity can come. And when it does — when honesty
rises — redemption is close behind.

**Your honesty about your gaps is not a threat to
your future.**

It is the doorway to it.

TODAY YOU WILL PLEDGE

Principle #4: Acknowledge the Gaps

(Hear this as truth spoken over your life today.)

You do not need to fear the truth that rises within you.

Honesty is not your enemy; it is your liberation.

You have the freedom to see the distance
between where you stand and where you long to be —
without condemning yourself for not being there yet.

The God who loves you meets you in that space between,
not with accusation, but with invitation.

You do not walk this road alone.

Seek the voices who will guide, steady, and strengthen
you.

Let clarity replace denial,
and humility replace pride.

Your gaps are not signs of defeat;
they are openings where growth can begin.

Embrace them with courage.

Face them with grace.

Build the bridges that will carry you forward,
one honest step at a time.

Acknowledge your gaps with truth and tenderness,
and open the doorway to your transformation.

Today you will.

Principle #5

You Are the Investment

You Are the Critical Piece
of Your Transformation

There comes a point in every journey of growth when the truth becomes unmistakably clear:

Your future will rise or fall on the investments you make in yourself.

Not the investments you make in your circumstances. Not the investments you make in your surroundings. But the investments you make in you — your mindset, your habits, your knowledge, your preparedness, your growth.

Ezra never understood this in his early life. He waited for circumstances to change. He waited for someone else to rescue him. He waited for transformation to arrive from the outside.

But transformation never comes from the outside.

Transformation begins the moment you recognize:

You are the vessel God will use to shape the future he is leading you toward.
You are the investment.

Everything you long for — your restored relationships, your renewed confidence, your desired achievements — will require something from you.

Not perfection.
Not proving yourself.
But investment.

Your future is not built on chance. It is built on choices. And each choice is a seed you sow into the person you are becoming.

This is your invitation to invest wisely, courageously, and continually into the life you desire to live.

The Power of Intentional Investment

There is no meaningful change without investment.

Every dream requires deposits.

Every transformation requires building.

Every breakthrough requires commitment.

The required investments may vary.

Perhaps you will need investments of time, talent, or treasure.

Other times will demand deposits of hope, determination, and resilience.

Some transformations require investments in personal development, education, and training.

And without doubt, every change will require courage, discipline, and the investment of a renewed mind.

Your mindset is not a small investment.

It is the foundation for all the others.

There are thoughts that strengthen you and thoughts that sabotage you.

There are beliefs that lift you and beliefs that quietly pull you back.

There is a voice within you that says, *"You can rise,"* and another that whispers, *"You will fall again."*

The voice you feed becomes the voice that leads.

Invest in the thoughts that build belief.

Invest in truths that remind you of who you
are becoming.
Invest in hope.
Invest in discipline.
Invest in the courage that refuses to quit.

Every investment you make in your mindset becomes a building block that strengthens the road beneath your feet.

Investments That Build the Bridge Forward

In the first three principles, you named your desired future, accepted responsibility for the outcomes, and designed the direction needed to get you there. In the fourth principle, you dared to acknowledge the gaps that must be crossed.

Now comes the work of building bridges to cross those gaps.

Some gaps can be crossed with simple, steady steps.

Others require a deeper commitment and a greater investment — training, education, healing, financial planning, new habits, new boundaries, new rhythms.

None of this is punishment.
None of this is failure.

This is simply the honest work needed to span the distance between where you stand and where you want to be.

Bridges are essential to close the gaps.

Bridges require intentional effort.

Bridges need investment.

And here is the quiet, freeing truth:

You do not need to fear the distance of the gap.
You only need to focus on the next investment
to lessen the gap.

Every investment strengthens the structure beneath you.

Every investment brings you closer to the life you desire.

Every investment builds the stamina you need for the journey ahead.

Your preferred future is not reached in a single action.

It is reached through consistent investments that shape the person you are becoming.

Why You Still Should Not Walk This Road Alone

As with every principle, transformation thrives in the presence of wise support.

Because even with the strongest intentions, you will face days when your resolve feels thin.

You will stumble.
You will face discouragement.
Old habits may return.
Old fears may echo.
Old doubts may rise.

And without support, these moments can feel like collapse.

But with trusted advisors—mentors, counselors, wise friends—the story is different.

They remind you that setbacks are not the end of your progress.

They help you see the structure you have already built.

They protect you from treating one stumble like a return to the beginning.

They steady your momentum when fear tries to pull you back.

They show you how to pick up the next building block and keep moving forward.

A trusted advisor knows that true transformation is not a fragile line of dominoes that falls with a single mistake.

**True transformation is a rising structure —
a foundation that grows stronger with each investment.**

They help you remember that every investment counts.

Every layer strengthens you.

Every step matters.

And nothing — nothing — about your journey is wasted.

Investment Requires Action

Everything in your journey has led you to this reality:

Desire alone cannot change your life.

Vision alone cannot change your life.

Hope alone cannot change your life.

Even a brilliant plan cannot change your life.

Only action can.

Action is the evidence of investment.

Action is the expression of belief.

Action is the step that tells heaven, "I am ready for what comes next."

You do not need perfect action.

You do not need dramatic action.

You only need faithful action —
the willingness to take the next step,
make the next investment,
place the next building block,
and trust that God is shaping the outcome as you move.

Your future will not arrive by waiting.

It will arrive by investing.

You are worth the investment.

Your purpose is worth the investment.

Your life is worth the investment.

**And today — not someday — is the place where
your investment begins.**

TODAY YOU WILL PLEDGE

Principle #5: You Are the Investment

*(Hear this spoken over your life
with strength and compassion.)*

You are not powerless, and you are not unprepared.

Your life is worthy of the investments that will carry you forward.

You have been given strength for the journey,
courage for the challenges,
and grace for the places where you will grow.

You are allowed to invest time, effort, resources,
and belief into the person you are becoming.

These investments are not selfish—
they are sacred.

They honor the purpose placed within you.

Feed the thoughts that strengthen you.

Today You Will

Nourish the hope that rises in you.

Protect your progress with wise voices beside you.

Do not fear the stumbles —
they cannot undo the foundation you are building.

Rise again.
Invest again.
Act again.

Your future draws nearer with every investment you make.

Your transformation unfolds each time you choose action over delay.

Remember that you are the investment.

Invest in yourself —
with courage, with consistency, with faith.

Today you will.

The Gift of Today

Lessons from Ian

I want to honor my son, Ian, in this final chapter. The twenty-six years of his life provide more than fond memories. He has left us with so much more.

There are moments in life when truth does not arrive through explanation.

It arrives through presence.

My son Ian taught us that.

Not through speeches.

Not through arguments.

Not through answers offered too quickly.

He taught us through how he lived —
and through how he faced the final days he was given.

———————

The Way He Lived

Ian did not wait on improvement.

He approached life with intention—seeking growth, learning, responsibility, and forward movement. He believed life was meant to be engaged, not postponed.

When something needed attention, he faced it. When something needed growth, he pursued it.

He did not live passively.

He lived deliberately.

And that posture never left him—not even at the end.

What Ian Taught Us About "Today"

Late on a Friday evening, we brought Ian home from the hospital. His medical team told us he had only days left. Home hospice care was arranged, and our family gathered around him.

On Saturday, hospice workers explained what the final physical signs would look like as his body began to shut down. Later that day, my wife and I, along with our other children, spoke privately with Ian about arrangements—cremation, funeral services, the things no parent ever wants to discuss with their child.

The conversation was honest.

And it was heavy.

That afternoon, our pastor came to the house. By then, more family had arrived—grandparents, aunts, uncles, cousins, nieces, nephews—filling the room where Ian rested.

Before the pastor arrived, I told him something had shifted in us. During the six months of Ian's battle with cancer, we had prayed for healing. Now, we felt called to stand near the finish line of Ian's race — not pleading for delay, but cheering him toward victory. We knew where Ian's trust rested.

During his conversation with Ian, our pastor spoke gently. He told Ian that a marathon is twenty-six miles long. He shared that he had run several himself, and that every race includes moments of pain, doubt, and exhaustion — moments when quitting feels easier than continuing.

But then he described the finish line.

He talked about crossing it.

The joy.

The release.

The celebration.

And then he said:

"Ian, maybe your life has been like a twenty-six-year marathon.

"You've run through some very difficult miles.

"Let me ask you the most important question
I can ask today."

He paused.

"If today were your last day, how confident are you — on
a scale of one to one hundred — that you would cross the
finish line of life and go to heaven?"

Ian did not hesitate.

"Ninety-eight percent."

The pastor smiled and asked why.

Ian answered simply:

"I believe the Bible is true.
"I believe Jesus did everything for me.
"There's nothing more I need to do to be right with God."

Then he paused and added,

"But isn't there always that two percent doubt?"

The pastor looked at him and said,
"I think you can move it up to one hundred."

There was no debate.

No correction needed.

Just clarity.

Peace Before the Pain

After that, the pastor asked one more question.

"Ian, what would you like me to pray for?"

Ian's answer came quietly — but firmly.

"Pray for peace.
"I don't want people questioning God.
"I don't want people asking why.
"I know God is good.
"And I know I'm good with God."

That request changed everything.

We had not yet faced the moment that would hurt the most. Ian had not yet taken his final breath. And we all knew that when that moment came, we would face a choice.

Not about faith.

About posture.

Would we become bitter —
or better?

Ian had already told us what he wanted.

Peace.

Trust.

No questioning of God's goodness.

He was telling us — before the pain arrived — how he hoped we would carry it.

The Choice Between Bitter and Better

Ian's request for peace led us directly into a conversation about choice.

Everyone who loved him would soon face a crossroads we never asked for — the same crossroads life eventually brings to us all:

Will this loss make us bitter,
or will it make us better?

Bitterness is quiet, but relentless.

It waits in the shadows, offering the illusion of protection while slowly stealing the life it promises to defend.

Better is harder at first.

It requires hope.

It requires trust when nothing makes sense.

Ezra and Malek stood on opposite sides of that
same choice.

One continued to mock.

One surrendered.

One clung to bitterness.

One reached toward better —
and found eternity waiting for him.

Ian's life brought that same decision to our doorstep.

And like Ezra, we discovered that even in sorrow,
there is a path toward goodness, growth,
and profound transformation.

No parent wants to become better through loss.

But we could honor Ian
by choosing the life he wanted for us —

a life marked by joy, trust, perseverance,
and gratitude for each today we are given.

Why This Book Exists

Ezra's story is not simply a parable.

It is a mirror.

It reflects every person who has ever paused long enough
to wonder:
whether change is possible,
whether growth can still happen,
whether the future can still be shaped differently than
the past.

For some, hope may feel distant.

For others, the weight of what has already been lived
may feel heavier
than the future they long for.

And Ian's story is the heartbeat
that makes this message personal.

He taught us — in fewer days than we expected —
that the power of today is not poetic.

It is practical.
It is urgent.
It is sacred.

You do not need a perfect history
to choose a better tomorrow.

You do not need certainty to take the next step.

You do not need a lifetime
to make your life meaningful.

You only need today.

This book exists because Ian reminded us of that truth
in a way we could never ignore.

His life called us to attention.

It asked us to be present.
It asked us to be grateful.
It asked us to be brave.

And it asked us — each in our own way —
to rise.

Your Life Will Be Measured in Todays

Your life will not be measured in decades.

Not in accomplishments.

Not in titles or achievements.

It will be measured
in the quiet accumulation of choices
made one day at a time.

Ezra understood this on the cross.

Ian embodied it in his life.

And now, the invitation is handed to you.

What will you do
with the today you have been given?
Will you drift toward what is familiar,
or rise toward the life
you were created to live?

Will you cling to bitterness,
or choose better—

the better that heals,
the better that grows,
the better that honors the people
and purposes entrusted to you?

You can claim the direction you desire.

You can begin the journey now.

Not someday.

Not tomorrow.

In this moment.

In this today.

That is the quiet promise woven through this book—
through Ezra's story,

and through Ian's life.

Today you will.

Acknowledgements

Some books are written alone.

This one was not.

Before any words were written,
before any story took shape,
this book rested on a truth larger than itself:

The greatest gap humanity has ever known
was bridged not by our effort or worthiness,
but by grace.

To my Creator —

the Author of redemption,
the source of courage,
and the One who revealed our value
by sending His only Son
to fulfill a plan we could not complete ourselves.

You offer hope that does not depend on our perfection,
but on Your faithfulness.

The principles in this book echo that truth.

To my family —

you walked with me through seasons of uncertainty,
loss, and reflection
with patience and honesty.

You carried strength when I did not have it,
and you gave this work the space it needed
to become what it was meant to be.

Your love made the journey possible.

To my friends —

you encouraged this work long before it was finished.
I specifically recognize **Mike Farragh**,
for teaching by example how to choose better instead of
bitter — even while facing ALS with courage, grace, and
resolve that continues to shape my own.

To my coach and mastermind group —

your voices of wisdom and counsel
helped shape clarity, challenge assumptions,
and protect the heart of the message.

Your guidance strengthened both the work
and the writer.

And to you, the reader —

thank you for giving this book your time and attention.

Thank you for walking with Ezra,
for considering the principles,
and for carrying Ian's story of courage
forward into your own life.

Today You Will

If these pages have helped you pause, reflect,
or move forward with greater intention,
then their purpose has been fulfilled.

May you honor the day you have been given.

May you choose what matters.

And may you trust that change —
quiet, faithful, and meaningful —
is possible.

Today you will.

In Loving Memory of
Ian Patrick Rasmussen

1997-2024

Ian Patrick Rasmussen entered this world on July 26, 1997, in the same Appleton home where he would take his final breath twenty-six years later, surrounded by family. He lived with intention, curiosity, and kindness—qualities that shaped not only his own life, but the lives of all who knew him.

Ian was the youngest son of Brian and Jill Rasmussen and a beloved brother, grandson, nephew, cousin — a devoted boyfriend and trusted friend. He carried a sharp mind and a generous heart.

He pursued learning with seriousness and joy, earning a degree in mathematics and computer science from the University of Wisconsin–Stevens Point and building a career at Esker, Inc. in software development marked by responsibility, growth, and excellence. Those who worked alongside him knew his thoughtfulness, his problem-solving ability, and his quiet leadership.

Ian loved competition and creativity in equal measure. He was known for his love of trivia, his skill and imagination as a Dungeon Master among friends, and his passion for music — teaching himself to play both piano and guitar. Volleyball was one of his great loves, and his relentless participation in tournaments across Wisconsin, Colorado, and Arizona connected him to a wide circle of friends who will forever remember his infectious smile and joyful competitiveness. He also cherished the outdoors, especially hiking, fly-fishing, and snowboarding.

Those who spent time with Ian knew his humor, his intelligence, and his steady presence. He was thoughtful without being showy, confident without arrogance, and deeply caring without seeking recognition. He built friendships wherever he went and left people better than he found them.

During a brief but fierce battle with renal medullary carcinoma, Ian continued to live with courage and clarity. In his final days, he offered a confession of faith that reflected the way he had lived — a trust not in his own effort, but in the finished work of Jesus Christ. He knew where his hope rested, and he was at peace with God.

One of Ian's final requests was simple and profound: that those he loved would choose peace and not question God's goodness. That request continues to guide his family and all who carry his memory forward.

Ian's life reminds us that meaning is not measured in length, but in how fully we show up for the days we are given.

About the Author

Brian Rasmussen is an author, speaker, and lifelong student of intentional living. *Today You Will* was shaped by personal reflection, lived experience, and the loss of his son, Ian—whose life and faith gave new meaning to the gift of each day. Brian writes to encourage readers to honor today with courage, clarity, and purpose.

Continuing the Journey

If the message of *Today You Will* resonated with you, it is likely because you recognize how often meaningful change is delayed — not for lack of desire, but because the present moment is crowded with responsibility, uncertainty, and competing demands.

Beyond the pages of this book, Brian Rasmussen continues this work in conversations, keynotes, and facilitated experiences designed to help individuals, leaders, and organizations navigate transition with clarity and intention. The principles shared here are applied in settings where growth, trust, and personal responsibility matter — whether in leadership teams, communities, or organizations facing change.

If you would like to continue the conversation or explore how the *Today You Will* framework might serve your context, you are welcome to learn more and connect at: **TodayLeadership.com.**

Wherever you lead next, may you do so with courage, clarity, and the resolve to honor today.